COMPETE OR

COOPERATE?

JD Savage

Illustrated by **James Gibbs**

Letter from the Author

There's a saying: horses for courses. It has nothing to do with eating horses, thankfully. It just means that different things suit different people. I hope you find an activity that suits you in this book.

I preferred individual sports as a boy: ones in which I competed as a single person. My favourite was cross-country running. We'd run across fields, along rivers, and through the countryside. We also had to clamber over gates and fences and steep, slippery hills made of mud. (Hey, maybe we invented parkour[1]!)

For me, it was a non-competitive activity. I just enjoyed being out in the fresh air, surrounded by nature. (OK, I wasn't so keen on the mud.)

I still run – and walk – for miles through green spaces today. It's a good way for writers to stay fit!

JD Savage

---

[1] a sport involving moving quickly over, under and around obstacles by running, jumping and climbing

Contents

Introduction 4

Animals that Compete 6

Animals that Cooperate 8

Competition and Cooperation at School 12

Dynamic Debate:
Is Competition Good for Kids? 14

Quiz: How Competitive Are *You*? 16

Competition and Cooperation in Sport 18

Major Sporting Events 28

Don't Like Sports? 32

Enter the Microworld 35

Compete or Cooperate? 38

Glossary 39

Index 40

The glossary

Some words in this book are in **bold**. When you read a **bold** word, think about what it means. If you don't know, you can look it up in the glossary at the end of the book.

Introduction

Competing is trying to be more successful than someone else – or lots of other people.

Cooperating is all about joining forces to get things done. It's when you work together for a common goal.

Competition might make us seem less friendly because it means working against each other. So why do we often choose competition over cooperation?

Some people think that competition is simply what life on Earth is all about. They compare us to the animals that constantly compete for food and survival. Only the winners survive! But is that really the lesson we take from nature?

Aren't **species** – including humans – more likely to survive if they cooperate?

Maybe we *should* take a closer look at the natural world ...

Animals that Compete

You'll certainly find plenty of competition in nature. Animals have many different ways of competing for **mates**.

Moose may clash antlers and have a shoving match.

Many male animals attract females by out-dancing their competitors. The male peacock spider waves its legs, and wiggles and waggles its body.

Even plants compete, for light, water, **minerals** and root space.

Lions and hyenas hunt the same prey and feed on the same animal remains. They compete for food on the African plains.

In south-eastern USA, meat-eating sundew plants catch insects on their sticky, sweet-smelling spines. Wolf spiders in the same region seem to understand that they must compete with the sundews for the same insects. They build larger webs than usual when sundews are nearby. Many insects end up in their webs instead of in the sundew traps!

So, *is* constant competition the natural order of things?

Animals that Cooperate

You may be surprised by just how many animals cooperate.

Monkeys and apes groom each other. That's cleaning each other's fur by removing dirt, **parasites**, plants and dried skin. It's a way of bonding, and it also helps to keep them healthy. Many other creatures groom each other, including squirrels, rats and horses.

That tickles!

Sea urchins hitch a lift on the backs of carrier crabs. The crabs get a spiky shield to use as a weapon if a **predator** approaches. The urchins get a ride to a new feeding ground.

It's a sea urchin, not a hair style.

If a vampire bat can't find blood to feed on for two nights running, it'll starve. To help, another bat will vomit up one of its own blood meals for the starving bat to eat. (And now *you* may feel sick, too.) Bats may help others because they know they might need help in return one day.

So I drink blood – get over it.

'Cleaner fish' feed on the dead skin and parasites (yum!) of bigger fish – including sharks. The fish get a meal and the shark keeps clean.

I like this new restaurant!

Ostriches and zebras often live by each other and travel together – for a good reason. Zebras have a great sense of smell and hearing but poor eyesight. Ostriches have great vision for spotting danger from afar but poor smell and hearing. When an ostrich or zebra becomes aware of a predator approaching, it flees. The rest of the herds follow.

We even see cooperation between insects and plants.

The acacia tree works closely with ants, pumping out a sugary sap that the ants love to eat. In return, the ants act as 'bodyguards' for the tree, fighting off caterpillars and other small predators. They'll even swarm onto the face of any giraffe that tries to eat the leaves, biting and stinging.

So, do you think species that cooperate stand a better chance of survival? Surely, if these creatures can cooperate, we can too. Yet it's hard to escape competition in the human world.

Competition and Cooperation at School

School is probably where you compete the most, especially when you play sports.

There's lots of competition in the classroom, too. After a test, you might compare scores with your classmates.

But what's better? Trying to beat others by pushing yourself to do better – or learning and developing skills at your own pace?

Some schools practise cooperative learning. The class gets broken down into small groups of pupils, who work together on a variety of projects. You and your group help each other to learn. If you're shy about putting your ideas forward, you may find it easier in a small group than in front of the whole class.

Which approach suits *you* best?

Dynamic Debate: Is Competition Good for Kids?

Let's look at the arguments for and against competing, to help you decide.

Yes – we like competing!

It's fun and keeps me fit.

It helps me to set goals, and winning gives me a reason to play.

If I lose, I can handle it. It motivates me to work harder.

It pushes me to do my best.

I love winning prizes. It means all my hard work got noticed.

I really like competing as a team. Winning as a team is the best!

No – we don't like competing!

It's not enough just to be good – you have to win. I hate the pressure.

Kids feel better when they work together instead of against each other.

I feel bad if I lose. Who doesn't?

Why do I need to compare myself with anyone else, anyway?

I prefer being friends than rivals.

Cooperating helps you to **appreciate** kids with different skills.

It's confusing: they're all good points! Let's find out which views you're more likely to share.

Quiz: How Competitive Are *You*?

Use a piece of paper to note down your answers to our totally scientific test. (Er, it's probably scientific. Well, it *might* be. OK, it isn't.)

How do you feel if you lose?

A. I pretend not to care – but I do really.
B. I feel angry and embarrassed.
C. I shrug it off and congratulate the winners.

How hard do you train for the sports you play?

A. I practise just as much as I need to.
B. I'm too busy training to answer this question!
C. Sports? What sports? I don't play sports.

What happens if a friend beats you at a video game?

A. I'll practise for hours before our next game.
B. I won't play it with them again.
C. Who cares? It's only a game.

Would you ever consider cheating at a sport?

A. Yes – but I wouldn't do it.
B. If I could get away with it, I would.
C. No: if you cheat you haven't really won.

If you play a game with a kid much younger than you, do you let them win?

A. Yes – unless I'm in a bad mood.
B. I'd have problems with that.
C. Yes – even if they're really bad at it!

Do grown-ups ever tell you to calm down when you're playing games?

A. I only get over-excited when everyone else does.
B. They have to tell me *every time*.
C. Calm down? Me? I couldn't be more relaxed.

If you answered:

Mostly As: You're quite competitive, but you've got it under control.
Mostly Bs: You're extremely competitive.
Mostly Cs: Maybe you prefer to cooperate.
All Bs: You're so competitive that you'll be pleased to hear you're the *most* competitive!

17

Competition and Cooperation in Sport

Cooperative sports

How do you feel about the cooperative approach to sport below? Do you love it – or does it sound all wrong to you? Think about whether you'd enjoy playing sports using these cooperative sports rules:

- Everyone gets to play, not just the best players.
- Everyone gets an equal amount of time playing.
- It's only about having fun and keeping fit.
- Nobody keeps score.
- There are no winners or losers!

Team sports

In team sports, you get to cooperate and compete at the same time. You cooperate with your teammates and compete against the opposing team.

In football, two teams of 11 players each try to score points by getting the ball into the other team's "GOOOOOOOALLLL!"

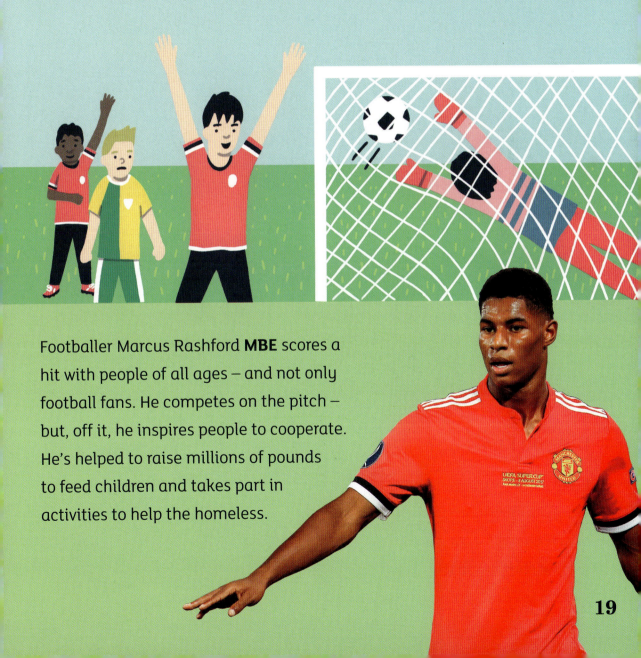

Footballer Marcus Rashford **MBE** scores a hit with people of all ages – and not only football fans. He competes on the pitch – but, off it, he inspires people to cooperate. He's helped to raise millions of pounds to feed children and takes part in activities to help the homeless.

Here are some more demanding team sports where you'll get a full-body workout.

Basketball involves many skills, including running, jumping and **hand-eye coordination**.

Did you know … ?

Basketball was originally played with a football and peach baskets. (They took the peaches out first!)

Lacrosse is a fast game in which players pass the ball to each other using a stick with a net at one end.

Would you believe … ?

Lacrosse was first played centuries ago by Native American tribes. As many as 1000 players took part on each side, the goals were miles apart, and the event could last for days.

In hockey, you try to get a puck or ball into the other team's goal using a stick – but remember to protect your shins from the other players' sticks too! Hockey has history. A similar game was played 4000 years ago by people in South America and Egypt.

Did you know … ?

In field hockey, players aren't allowed to play left-handed. There's a higher risk of people getting hit if left-handed sticks are combined with right-handed sticks.

What's so good about team sports, then?

Team sports will help you develop teamwork skills, as you learn how to work well with others. You may be inspired to give your absolute best efforts for your teammates. You'll also share responsibility for the final score – so it's not all on *your* shoulders.

Some kids would enjoy team sports, except for one thing: the **ball-hogs** on their team. These players rarely pass to other players, leaving the rest of the team standing around for an hour not doing anything. Yaaaaaaawn.

It's one reason why some kids prefer ...

... Individual sports

These are sports in which you compete as an individual rather than as a team member. They may suit you if you prefer not to rely on other people's skills – or don't like being in a group.

They include:

Tennis: Players score points by hitting the ball so their opponents can't hit it back over the net.

Golf: Players try to hit their balls into a series of holes with as few strokes as possible.

Wrestling: This combat sport involves using your body strength to force your opponent to the ground – but you need proper coaching to avoid injury.

Did you know … ?

Wrestling may be the world's oldest combat sport. The ancient Greeks and ancient Egyptians wrestled.

Skateboarding: This one's for kids who like competitions of skill, speed and daring. Skateboarders ride a wooden board around a skatepark at high speed and do difficult tricks in the air!

These sports allow you to develop skills at your own pace. Remember, though: you can't hide in a crowd of players – all eyes will be on you!

Non-competitive sports

(They're competitive only if you *want* them to be.)

Parkour is about training your body to move freely through any environment. The skills used to **navigate** obstacles include running, jumping, climbing, rolling and tumbling – whatever it takes! Some parkour athletes also add flips and spins to express themselves. If you want to try parkour, you should always start out in a class with proper coaching, to learn how to do it safely and correctly.

Swimming helps to build **endurance** and muscle strength, and helps keep your heart healthy. You don't even need full use of your limbs to be a good swimmer. Floating in water can give a real sense of freedom for all athletes, including those with limited movement.

Running is excellent exercise – which makes you feel great, too. You could aim to achieve a 'personal best' (your best result) – or just run for fun!

"Don't dream of winning, train for it." **Sir Mo Farah CBE**, British long-distance runner and Olympic gold medalist

Major Sporting Events

The Olympic Games

We know the Olympic Games were held as early as 776 **BCE** in Ancient Greece at a site called Olympia (and now you know how they got their name!) After Emperor Theodosius banned them in about 393 **CE**, they took a massive break of over 1500 years. They were finally brought back in 1896.

Now the Olympics is the world's leading sports event, with athletes from over 200 countries taking part. There are Summer Games and Winter Games, with two years between them. They're each held every four years in a different country.

The colours of the Olympic rings represent America, Asia, Africa, Europe and Australia – but why isn't the continent of Antarctica represented? Guess, and then check the answer below.

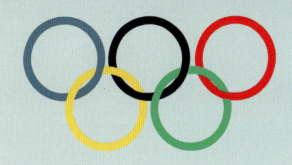

The Games include some cooperation, as well as competition. For each Olympics, a flame is lit in Olympia and becomes the Olympic Torch. A number of runners, one passing it to another, must carry it all the way to the country hosting the games that year. The flame must not go out, despite the weather.

Fortunately for them, they don't have to swim from country to country with it! When it can't be carried on foot, it's transported on a plane.

Antarctica isn't represented because it hasn't yet put together an Olympic team. Don't be too surprised: almost all of Antarctica's human inhabitants are scientists doing research projects (and the penguins living there aren't too keen on sports).

29

Sports star spotlight

Classic science-fiction film *E.T. the Extra-Terrestrial* got Sir Chris Hoy MBE interested in bikes as a boy. Seeing its alien star ride across the sky on a BMX bike inspired him to buy one – for £5 from a jumble sale!

He grew up and went on to win seven Olympic medals (including six gold) and 11 world championships as a cyclist. After that, he wrote the *Flying Fergus* children's books to inspire other kids to cycle.

The Paralympic Games

The Paralympic Games are a major international sports event in which disabled people compete. Sports range from fencing to skiing. They take place just after the Olympic Games.

Passionate snowboarder Amy Purdy lost both of her legs due to **meningitis**, aged 19. She challenged herself to achieve things that even people with two legs would find difficult. She went on to win several World Cup gold medals in snowboard-cross and become the top-ranked para-snowboarder in the USA.

Don't Like Sports?

Some kids dislike sports for various reasons. The risk of injury may put them off, or they may simply have no interest. No rule says you *must* like sports! (Honestly, we checked.)

You can still be active. If you're a nature lover, you may prefer rambling. That's walking outdoors, where you can explore nature – and compete *or* cooperate. You can compete to be the first to discover animals and plants, or work with others to do those things.

Alternative activities

If you don't like school sports, would you change your mind if you could choose one of these sports to play?

- video games
- robot combat
- rolling down hills
- underwater cycling
- marbles
- finger wrestling
- rock-paper-scissors
- worm charming

Worm charming is a sport in which every competitor is given an area of ground. They must attract as many worms out of it as they can, by tapping on it and making vibrations. It's also called worm grunting. (It's not harmful to the worms.)

Keep the noise down!

Cooperative board games

If you prefer to cooperate when you play, you may be interested in cooperative board games. These are about group problem-solving, and you must cooperate to win.

Game designer Matt Leacock has created many games where everyone is on the same team, and you all win or lose together. He wants everyone to feel good after playing his games – even if they lose.

Younger kids can even play some of the games aimed at slightly older players because they're so cooperative. Older players can help them out.

Enter the Microworld

Whether or not you like competing, there's lots of competing going on deep inside you right now!

Did you know that you're only about 43% human? The rest of you is a microbiome. That's the name for the trillions of microbes living inside you. Microbes are the tiniest and simplest known forms of life and mainly live in the gut. They help to break down the food you eat, fight infections, and help you stay healthy – and they are *very* competitive.

Scientists once thought that these microbes were all cooperating to keep us healthy. Now they feel sure that they're competing.

Some microbes can divide and double their numbers in just 20 minutes. So, you can imagine the competition going on inside your gut – for food, space and oxygen. The food you put into your body decides which bacteria win that competition.

Different bacteria survive on different foods. The bacteria that keep us healthy seem to love the fibre found in plant foods.

No two people's gut biomes are the same, but when we eat high-fibre foods like fruit, vegetables, beans, nuts and wholegrains, we seem to add to the 'good' bacteria. This means you can help the 'invisible army' of bacteria that keeps you healthy to win the competition every time you eat.

Compete or Cooperate?

So ... is one better than the other? Are they even opposites?

Competing pushes and challenges us – but we develop skills and challenge ourselves when we cooperate, too. And when we cooperate, winning doesn't mean coming first or beating everyone else, because we win as a team. As we've learned though, life is full of competition. It's hard to avoid, and many of us enjoy it.

Maybe we need both in our lives – and to strike a healthy balance between the two!

Glossary

appreciate: to be grateful for something

ball-hogs: players in sport who refuse to pass a ball to teammates

BCE (Before Common Era): before year 1

CBE: an honour awarded by the monarch of the UK to people who make a great positive impact in their work

CE (Common Era): after year 1

endurance: the ability to continue for a long time

hand-eye coordination: the way that someone's hands and sight work together

mates: partners with which to produce young animals

MBE: an honour awarded by the monarch of the UK to people who make a positive impact in their work

meningitis: a serious disease that causes swelling around the brain and spinal cord

minerals: substances that provide growth and energy (plants get minerals from soil)

navigate: to travel over, through or around

parasites: animals or plants that live on or in another animal or plant, getting food from it

predator: an animal that hunts and kills other animals for food

species: a group of animals or plants with certain characteristics in common

Index

acacia tree 11

basketball 20

carrier crabs 8

cleaner fish 9

Farah, Mo 27

football 19

hockey 22

Hoy, Chris 30

lacrosse 21

Leacock, Matt 34

Olympic Games 28–30

Paralympic Games 31

parkour 26

peacock spider 6

Purdy, Amy 31

Rashford, Marcus 19

sea urchins 8

sundew 7

vampire bat 9

wolf spider 7